EXTRA FOCUS ADHD:

A Powerful Guide Navigating the Storm of ADHD in Adults

KPC HEALTH PUBLISHERS

imply any affiliation with or endorsement by the trademark owners.

For my family and everyone who seeks to understand and conquer ADHD.

INTRODUCTION

ADHD Extra Focus: A Practical Guide "Navigating the Storm of ADHD in Adults" is a comprehensive resource designed to assist individuals with Attention Deficit Hyperactivity Disorder (ADHD) in better understanding, managing, and thriving in the face of the challenges offered by this neurodevelopmental disorder. This comprehensive book looks into the nuances of adult ADHD and offers practical tactics, resources, and insights to improve attention, productivity, and general well-being.

Understanding Adult ADHD

A description of adult ADHD, including its prevalence, symptoms, and influence on everyday living.

The distinctions between childhood and adult ADHD.

ADHD's neurological basis and how it impacts cognitive functions.

Chapter 2: Diagnosis and Evaluation

The significance of receiving expert diagnosis and evaluation.

A breakdown of the adult ADHD diagnosis criteria.

Methods for locating the best healthcare provider and obtaining an accurate diagnosis.

Medication and Treatment Options (Chapter 3)

An examination of pharmacological choices routinely used to treat adult ADHD.

Non-pharmacological therapies, such as counselling, lifestyle adjustments, and dietary considerations, are discussed.

Advice on how to manage medications and their adverse effects.

Chapter 4: Practical ADHD Management Strategies

Techniques for better time management and organization.

Distraction-reduction and focus-intensification techniques.

The importance of mindfulness and meditation in ADHD treatment.

Tips for staying motivated and avoiding procrastination.

Building Support Systems (Chapter 5)

The significance of forming a support network that includes friends, family, and professionals.
Techniques for explaining your ADHD needs to others.
Adults with ADHD might benefit from support groups and internet networks.
Chapter 6: Managing Your Work and Career

Time management, organization, and communication are examples of workplace success strategies.
Options for disclosure and accomodation for people with ADHD.
Career options that complement ADHD talents and interests.
Relationship Management (Chapter 7)

Tips for sustaining good relationships in the face of ADHD-related difficulties.
Communication techniques for explaining ADHD to family members.

Identifying and avoiding typical relationship hazards connected with ADHD.
Self-Care and Wellness (Chapter 8)

Adults with ADHD must prioritize self-care.
Stress, anxiety, and concomitant disorders management strategies.
Making exercise, diet, and sleep a part of an ADHD-friendly lifestyle.
Thriving with ADHD, Chapter 9

Stories of people who have achieved success and joy while having ADHD.
Tips for accepting and utilizing the distinct qualities linked with ADHD.
The path to self-acceptance and resilience.
Conclusion: "Extra Focus ADHD: A Powerful Guide Navigating the Storm of ADHD in Adults" is a useful resource that enables individuals with ADHD to take charge of their life, effectively manage their symptoms, and realize their full

potential. This book, which combines professional insights, practical methods, and inspirational anecdotes, offers as a light of hope for anyone navigating the often difficult seas of adult ADHD.

CHAPTER 1: UNDERSTANDING ADHD IN ADULTS

The chapter "Understanding ADHD in Adults" is expected to discuss the frequently misunderstood condition of Attention-Deficit/Hyperactivity Disorder (ADHD) in adults. Although ADHD is often associated with children, it can linger into adults and create distinct issues. This chapter looks at how ADHD affects adults, including symptoms, diagnosis, impact on everyday living, and potential treatment choices.

Diagnosis and Symptoms:

Adult ADHD symptoms include trouble concentration, impulsivity, restlessness, and executive function deficiencies.

Adult ADHD diagnostic criteria may differ from those for children, although they frequently involve a history of symptoms that have persisted beyond childhood.

Comprehensive examinations, including as interviews, self-report questionnaires, and medical history evaluation, are often used to make a diagnosis.

The Effect on Daily Life:

The chapter might go through how ADHD impacts several parts of adult life, such as job, relationships, and personal well-being.

Organization, time management, and concentration issues can make it difficult to have a stable career, meet deadlines, and maintain good relationships.

Co-occurring Disorders:

ADHD is frequently associated with other mental health issues such as anxiety, depression, and drug misuse. These links and their ramifications may be explored in the chapter.

Treatment Alternatives:

Adult ADHD treatment may include a combination of behavioral therapy, medication, and lifestyle changes.

To control symptoms, medications such as stimulants (e.g., methylphenidate) and non-stimulants (e.g., atomoxetine) may be administered.

Individuals might benefit from behavioral therapy to build coping mechanisms and enhance executive function abilities.

Stigma and Public Awareness:

The chapter may discuss the stigma associated with adult ADHD, as well as how improved knowledge and understanding may help to lessen stigma and create better support for people with this illness. Conclusion: Understanding ADHD in adults is critical for proper diagnosis and management. This chapter is likely to give significant insights into the difficulties that individuals with ADHD confront, the need of early diagnosis, and the variety of treatment choices available to enhance their quality of life. It may also underline the importance of empathy and support for people living with ADHD.

CHAPTER 2 DIAGNOSIS AND ASSESSMENT IN ADULTHOOD

Introduction: The "Diagnosis and Assessment in Adulthood" chapter generally dives into the numerous methods and concerns involved in measuring adults' psychological, emotional, and mental health. This chapter is essential for professionals in psychology, psychiatry, counseling, and social work because it gives insights for understanding and evaluating the well-being of adult clients.

Assessment Overview:

The chapter frequently starts with an introduction of the relevance of adult assessment, highlighting its role in recognizing mental health illnesses, understanding personal strengths and limitations, and directing treatment choices.

Tools and Techniques for Assessment:

It addresses a variety of assessment procedures and approaches, including structured interviews, self-report questionnaires, psychological testing (such as personality assessments and intelligence tests), and behavioral observations.
Interviews with Clinicians:

Clinical interviews, which entail face-to-face exchanges between the therapist and the client, are covered in detail. This section may offer advice on how to create rapport, ask open-ended inquiries, and obtain relevant information.
Psychological Evaluation:

The aim and administration of several psychological tests used in maturity examinations, as well as their validity and reliability, are explained. The MMPI-2, Beck Depression Inventory, and cognitive evaluation tools are among examples.
Considerations for Culture:

The need of addressing cultural elements in evaluation is emphasized. This section addresses how people' perceptions of health and mental well-being might be influenced by their cultural background.

SPECIFIC DISORDER EVALUATION:

Sections of the chapter may be devoted to assessing certain mental health illnesses common in adults, such as depression, anxiety, bipolar disorder, and personality disorders. It describes the diagnostic criteria as well as the testing techniques for each disease.

Ethical and legal concerns:

Addresses the ethical concerns and legal requirements associated with adult evaluation. This includes concerns about confidentiality, informed consent, and the use of evaluation results in court. Assessment in a Variety of Populations:

Discusses evaluation procedures for a variety of demographics, including LGBTQ+ people, older persons, and people with impairments.
Treatment Planning Assessment:

The importance of evaluation in generating tailored treatment programs is highlighted. It investigates how assessment findings influence treatment options such as therapy techniques, medication, or lifestyle changes.
Future Trends and Challenges:

Examines assessment difficulties, such as resistance to diagnosis or treatment, as well as developing trends in assessment methodology, such as the use of technology and telemedicine.
Conclusion: The chapter finishes by summarizing the key topics raised and emphasizing the continuing necessity of competent diagnosis and

evaluation in supporting adult mental health and well-being.

CHAPTER 3: TITLE UNMASKING THE MYTHS OF ADHD

The chapter "Unmasking the Myths of ADHD" is likely to begin with an introduction that sets the tone for the debate. It may stress the incidence and effect of ADHD (Attention-Deficit/Hyperactivity Disorder) and the need of dispelling myths about the illness.

Myth: ADHD Is simply a Childhood condition: This section will address the common fallacy that ADHD is simply a childhood condition. It would go through how ADHD may remain into adulthood, affecting numerous elements of a person's life such as school, career, and relationships.

Myth: ADHD Is Just a Lack of attention: This chapter will debunk the myth that ADHD is just characterized by a lack of attention. It would dive into the disorder's complexities, highlighting symptoms such as impulsivity, hyperactivity, and executive functioning problems.

Myth: ADHD is Overdiagnosed and Overmedicated: This section may address the debate around the apparent overdiagnosis and overmedication of ADHD, while also offering evidence-based information regarding acceptable diagnosis and treatment standards.

Myth: ADHD is caused by bad parenting or laziness:
Addressing the stigmatizing ideas about ADHD, this section of the chapter would emphasize that ADHD is a neurological illness that is not caused by poor parenting, laziness, or a lack of discipline.

Myth: Medication Is the Only Treatment Option: This session would go through the many ADHD treatment techniques, emphasizing that medication is only one component of a full treatment strategy.

As helpful interventions, it would suggest behavioral treatment, lifestyle adjustments, and accommodations.

Myth: ADHD Is the Same for Everyone: This section would emphasize the variety of ADHD by addressing how symptoms and severity can differ between individuals. It may also address the various subtypes of ADHD, such as mainly inattentive, predominantly hyperactive-impulsive, and combination presentation.

Myth: ADHD is not a legitimate medical condition:

To address certain people's concern regarding ADHD's legitimacy as a medical diagnosis, this section of the chapter would include empirical data supporting its neurological foundation, such as brain imaging and genetic research.

Conclusion: The chapter would close by summarizing the main points and emphasizing the need of debunking stereotypes about ADHD in order to promote understanding, eliminate stigma, and ensure that people with ADHD receive adequate support and treatment.

CHAPTER 4 "MANAGING EXECUTIVE FUNCTION CHALLENGES.

Executive functions are a set of cognitive abilities that allow people to plan, organize, and begin tasks, maintain attention, manage time, and regulate emotions. These functions are critical for goal-directed behavior and success in a variety of areas of life, including job, school, and daily activities.

The following major principles may be found in a chapter on handling executive function challenges:

Introduction to Executive Functions: The chapter will most likely begin with familiarizing readers with the notion of executive functions. It would clarify that executive functions include a variety of abilities such as working memory, cognitive flexibility, inhibitory control, and others.

Common Executive Function issues: This chapter will go over some of the most common executive function issues that people confront. Planning, organization, time management, task commencement, and impulse control are examples of these obstacles.

Causes and Development: Readers will learn about the possible causes of executive function problems. This may include neurological variables, such as disparities in brain growth, as well as contextual influences that might impact the development of executive functions.

The chapter would illustrate how executive function issues might affect numerous elements of a person's life. This might range from scholastic issues in school to employment, interpersonal, and daily routine obstacles.

Assessment and Diagnosis: This chapter may go into detail on how experts assess and diagnose executive function issues. Standardized tests, interviews, and observations may be used to determine the level of the issues.

methods and Interventions: A substantial amount of the chapter would be devoted to methods and interventions for dealing with executive function issues. This might include practical approaches and advice for increasing executive function abilities. Using visual aids, forming routines, setting objectives, and applying self-regulation skills are some examples.

Educational and Therapeutic techniques: The chapter may explore educational and therapeutic techniques that can be beneficial for those who struggle with executive function. This might include special education, occupational therapy, or cognitive-behavioral treatment procedures.

Support Systems: The chapter would most likely stress the need of a robust support system, which includes parents, teachers, and professionals, in assisting persons with executive function problems to succeed. Strategies for collaboration and communication among various parties should be investigated.

Case Studies: Real-life case studies or personal tales on how people overcame executive function issues may be included. These examples can serve as both inspiration and practical guidance.

Future areas: The chapter might finish with a discussion of future research areas as well as upcoming technologies or therapies that have the potential to improve executive function skills.

A chapter on managing executive function difficulties would essentially try to give a full explanation of these crucial cognitive skills, their impact, and practical suggestions for effectively resolving them. The amount and level of material in such a chapter would be determined by the context of the book or resource in which it appears.

CHAPTER 5
MEDICATION OPTIONS AND CONSIDERATIONS FOR ADHD PATIENTS.

Overview of the Chapter:

The chapter "Medication Options and Considerations for ADHD Patients" is an essential part of any comprehensive handbook or textbook on Attention-Deficit/Hyperactivity Disorder (ADHD). This chapter goes into the numerous pharmacological therapies for ADHD symptoms, examining their methods of action, potential side effects, and variables to consider when prescribing these drugs.

Key Medication Alternatives:

Stimulant drugs: The most usually recommended drugs for ADHD are stimulants. They function by boosting the levels of specific neurotransmitters in the brain, particularly dopamine and norepinephrine. Methylphenidate-based pharmaceuticals (e.g., Ritalin, Concerta) and amphetamine-based drugs (e.g., Adderall, Vyvanse) are examples of common stimulant medications.

Non-stimulant drugs are frequently tried when stimulants are ineffective or cause unpleasant side effects. Atomoxetine (Strattera), guanfacine (Intuniv), and clonidine (Kapvay) are a few examples.

Consider the following factors:

Patient Age and Specific Symptoms: Medication selection can be influenced by the patient's age as well as specific ADHD symptoms. Children and adults, for example, may react differently to specific drugs, and certain medications may be more helpful at managing inattention while others are more effective at tackling hyperactivity and impulsivity.

Comorbidity: ADHD patients frequently have comorbid illnesses including anxiety, depression, or oppositional defiant disorder. Medication selection should take these comorbidities into account in order to provide a holistic therapeutic strategy.

Patient Response and Tolerance: It is critical to monitor the patient's response to medicine. To determine the correct dosage and composition for each individual, adjustments may be required. Some people may develop adverse effects that necessitate prescription adjustments.

Duration of effect: The duration of effect of medications varies. Short-acting formulations may require repeated doses throughout the day, but long-acting versions provide prolonged coverage and ease.

Medication alternatives may have adverse effects ranging from appetite suppression and sleep disruptions to elevated heart rate and blood pressure. Healthcare practitioners must take these into account when prescribing and monitor patients for negative effects.

Stimulant drugs have the potential for misuse or abuse, especially in teenagers and young adults. Prescribers must carefully analyze the risk and educate patients and their families on how to take these drugs responsibly.

Medication Breaks: Some patients benefit from medication breaks, in which they take pauses from their medicine to reduce tolerance and potential negative effects.

Conclusion: The chapter on "Medication Options and Considerations for ADHD Patients" is an essential resource for healthcare professionals and people who suffer from ADHD. It highlights the necessity of personalizing therapy to the individual's needs, closely monitoring drug response, and taking into account a variety of factors in order to obtain best results in treating ADHD symptoms while reducing potential dangers and side effects.

CHAPTER 6 COGNITIVE BEHAVIORAL STRATEGIES FOR ADHD.

Cognitive Behavioral Therapy (CBT) is a well-known treatment for attention deficit/hyperactivity disorder (ADHD) and its accompanying difficulties. This chapter will most likely dig into the following major points:

Understanding ADHD: The chapter would begin with defining ADHD and its primary symptoms, which include inattention, hyperactivity, and impulsivity. It may also emphasize how ADHD might interfere with daily activities such as academic achievement, job, and relationships.

The CBT Approach: It would introduce the concept of Cognitive Behavioral Therapy, focusing on its purpose of assisting people with ADHD in better understanding their thoughts, feelings, and actions. Because of its evidence-based approach, CBT is a helpful tool in ADHD management.

Identification of Negative thinking Patterns: CBT frequently begins with the identification of negative thinking patterns or cognitive distortions that can aggravate ADHD symptoms. Perfectionism, self-criticism, and a propensity to catastrophize are examples.

Behavioral methods: The chapter would go over particular behavioral methods utilized in ADHD CBT. Techniques such as time management, organizational skills, setting realistic objectives, and building routines to boost attention and productivity should be included.

Managing Impulsivity: Impulsivity is a typical issue for people with ADHD. CBT can teach skills for pausing and thinking before acting, so improving decision-making and impulse control.

Mindfulness and Self-Regulation: The chapter may go through how mindfulness practices might assist people with ADHD in being more aware of their thoughts and emotions. Improved self-regulation and emotional control can result from increased self-awareness.

Social Skills Training: Social connections can be difficult for those with ADHD. CBT can help people improve their communication skills, empathy, and develop healthier relationships.

Homework and Practice: CBT frequently includes homework assignments that urge people to apply what they've learned in real-life settings. These tasks serve to reinforce the skills and tactics that were addressed in treatment.

pharmaceutical Complement: While the chapter focuses mostly on non-pharmacological therapies, it may also describe how CBT might supplement pharmaceutical treatments for ADHD by providing a comprehensive approach to symptom management.

Monitoring Progress: The chapter may stress the need of tracking progress over time. Regular assessments and feedback assist individuals and therapists in determining the efficacy of CBT therapies and making appropriate modifications.

Coping with Difficulties: Finally, the chapter may discuss frequent obstacles that people with ADHD may have throughout CBT and provide advice on how to overcome setbacks and stay motivated.

Overall, the chapter on "Cognitive Behavioral Strategies for ADHD" gives a thorough review of how CBT may be a useful tool in treating the symptoms and issues associated with ADHD. It would attempt to provide people with ADHD with practical skills and methods for improving their everyday functioning and quality of life.

CHAPTER 7 BUILDING EFFECTIVE HABITS AND ROUTINES FOR ADHD.

Individuals suffering with Attention Deficit Hyperactivity Disorder (ADHD) frequently struggle with attention, organization, and time management. Developing efficient habits and routines can substantially aid in dealing with these issues. Here are a few examples of frequent tactics described in such chapters:

Understanding ADHD: The chapter will most likely start with a definition of ADHD and how it affects attention, impulsivity, and executive functioning. Before implementing tactics, it is critical to first understand the condition.

Goal Setting: It is critical to set specific and attainable goals. These objectives should be broken down into smaller, more attainable tasks to make them less intimidating.

Time Management: Time management is critical. Timers, calendars, and to-do lists, for example, can assist people with ADHD keep on track.

Creating a pattern: Establishing a defined daily pattern can give predictability. This might include specific hours for work, food, exercise, and rest.

Prioritization: Knowing how to prioritize work is essential. The chapter may go through approaches for identifying and prioritizing high-priority jobs.

Distraction Reduction: Strategies for limiting environmental distractions, such as shutting off alerts and maintaining a clutter-free workstation, can be quite beneficial.

Mindfulness and meditation can assist people with ADHD enhance their attention and self-awareness, as well as reduce impulsivity.

Medication and treatment: The chapter may also discuss the function of medication and treatment (such as Cognitive Behavioral Therapy) in ADHD symptoms management.

Self-Care: The value of self-care in ADHD management should not be underestimated. This includes getting adequate sleep, eating a balanced food, and exercising on a regular basis.

Flexibility and Self-Compassion: The chapter may emphasize the necessity of flexibility and self-forgiveness in the face of failures. ADHD treatment is an ongoing practice that requires patience and kindness toward oneself.

Building a support network, including friends, family, and maybe support groups, can be useful for those with ADHD.

Tracking Progress: The chapter may suggest maintaining a notebook or utilizing apps to track progress and highlight areas where habits and routines might be changed.

Keep in mind that exact tactics and recommendations will differ based on the author and the context of the book or resource. Individuals with ADHD should consult with healthcare specialists or therapists who can give specialized counsel and assistance tailored to their specific requirements.

CHAPTER 8
NAVIGATING RELATIONSHIPS AND SOCIAL CHALLENGES FOR ADHD PATIENTS.

This chapter is likely to cover many elements of ADHD (Attention-Deficit/Hyperactivity Disorder) and how it might affect a person's ability to form and maintain relationships, as well as cope with social obstacles. Please keep in mind that, while I can offer a basic summary, the particular substance of such a chapter may differ depending on the source or book from which it is derived. Here's a breakdown of what you may discover in a chapter like this:

Introduction to ADHD: The chapter might start with an introduction to ADHD, outlining what it is and its main features, which include difficulty with attention, impulsivity, and hyperactivity. This section may also address the societal prevalence of ADHD.

ADHD's Social Implications: It would most likely go into how ADHD might impact an individual's social life. This might include having difficulties focusing during talks, being impulsive in social circumstances, and having problems managing time for social responsibilities.

Building connections: The chapter may investigate the difficulties that ADHD persons have while attempting to create and maintain personal and professional connections. This might include difficulty actively listening, forgetfulness, and impulsivity in personal relationships.

Impact on Family Relationships: There may be a section on how ADHD affects family relations. It may address the stress that caregivers or family members may feel while dealing with an ADHD individual, as well as ways for enhancing family ties.

Relationships at School and Work: The influence of ADHD on academic and work-related relationships may also be considered. This might involve disagreements with students, instructors, coworkers, and superiors.

Coping techniques: The chapter will most likely include practical techniques and coping processes for people with ADHD to manage social barriers and create stronger connections. Tips on time management, communication skills, and self-regulation strategies may be included.

Medication and treatment: Information on the role of medication and treatment in the management of ADHD symptoms and the improvement of social interactions may be provided. This might include examining the advantages and disadvantages of ADHD drugs, as well as the efficiency of other methods of therapy.

Support Systems: The value of a support system for both the person with ADHD and their loved ones cannot be overstated. This might include therapists', support groups', and educational resources' roles.

Personal tales and Case Studies: Some chapters may incorporate personal tales or case studies of people with ADHD and their struggles with social problems. These real-life examples might offer relevant insights and inspiration.

Conclusion: The chapter might end by summarizing significant insights and underlining the significance of recognizing and dealing with the social components of ADHD.

CHAPTER 9 :ADHD CAREER STRATEGIES"

However, I can provide some basic suggestions on job strategy for those with ADHD:

Understanding ADHD: The chapter will most likely start with discussing what ADHD is, what its symptoms are, and how it might impair a person's work life. It might go through the many varieties of ADHD and how they appear in an adult's work life.

Self-Acceptance and Awareness: Individuals with ADHD must accept themselves and become aware of their own strengths and flaws. This self-awareness can help people manage their professions more effectively.

Time Management and Organization: Those with ADHD may find it difficult to manage their time and keep organized. The chapter may include tactics and tools for enhancing these abilities, such as the use of calendars, to-do lists, and time-blocking approaches.

Setting Achievable objectives: Setting attainable objectives and breaking them down into smaller, manageable activities can help people with ADHD stay focused and motivated.

Work Environment: The necessity of building a favorable work environment may be discussed in the chapter. This involves reducing distractions, maximizing workspace arrangement, and, if required, finding accommodations.

Communication Skills: In the business, effective communication is essential. Communication strategies for both peers and supervisors may be explored.

Stress Management: ADHD may be stressful, particularly in high-pressure settings at work. The chapter might go through stress-reduction approaches like mindfulness or relaxation exercises.

Medication and Treatment: Some people with ADHD benefit from medication and counseling. The chapter might include information about various treatment alternatives and how they can be incorporated into a career plan.

Networking and Support: Having a support network of friends, family, or coworkers that understand ADHD may be quite beneficial. The chapter might go through the advantages of obtaining help and interacting with people who are going through similar things.

Finally, the chapter may discuss selecting a professional path that matches with one's talents and interests. Certain occupations may be more accommodating to people with ADHD than others.

CHAPTER 10 FINANCIAL MANAGEMENT AND ADHD

as of my most recent knowledge update in September 2021, in any generally known academic or reference works. It's possible that such a chapter or topic has appeared after my last update, or that it's a specialist subject in a certain book or journal.

However, I can offer some broad facts on the relationship between financial management and ADHD:

Understanding Attention Deficit Hyperactivity condition (ADHD): Attention Deficit Hyperactivity Disorder (ADHD) is a neurodevelopmental condition characterized by symptoms such as difficulties paying attention, impulsivity, and hyperactivity. It has an impact on people's capacity to concentrate, manage work, and make smart judgments.

Financial Difficulties: Because of their cognitive and behavioral characteristics, people with ADHD may experience specific financial issues. These obstacles might include budgetary difficulties, impulsive spending, and organizational and paperwork difficulties.

Impulsivity and Spending: Impulsivity is a prevalent problem. People with ADHD may make hasty financial decisions, such as buying unnecessary purchases or incurring debt without considering the long-term implications. This can result in financial insecurity.

Budgeting and Planning: ADHD can make it difficult to set and adhere to a budget. They may struggle to organize financial papers, manage spending, and make financial objectives.

Time Management: Time management is extremely important in financial planning. ADHD can impair one's ability to manage time efficiently, resulting in missed bill payments, deadlines, or financial adviser visits.

Seeking specialist intervention: Managing money with ADHD may necessitate the intervention of a specialist. Financial advisers that understand ADHD can assist in developing specific solutions to manage these issues.

Medication and Therapy: For some people with ADHD, medication and therapy assist them manage their symptoms, which can enhance their money management abilities.

Education and Support: Individuals and their families require ADHD knowledge and education. Support groups and educational resources can help with money management skills and coping processes.

Technology and Tools: There are a variety of financial management applications and tools available to assist people with ADHD in staying organized and tracking their finances more successfully.

Long-Term preparation: Despite the difficulties, people with ADHD may achieve financial stability and success with careful preparation, support systems, and a dedication to managing their particular financial demands.

If you have access to the exact chapter you referenced, or if you'd need more thorough information on a similar issue, please share more specifics or questions, and I'll do my best to help you further.

CHAPTER 12
SELF-CARE AND
EMOTIONAL
WELL-BEING.

However, because the topic of self-care and emotional well-being may contain a vast variety of material, I'll need additional background concerning the precise content and aims of this chapter.

In general, a chapter like this in a book or instructional material would contain themes like:

Self-Care Introduction: This section should begin with defining self-care and its relevance in preserving emotional well-being. It might also talk about the distinctions between physical, emotional, and mental self-care.

Self-Assessment: In order to conduct self-care successfully, individuals must first understand their own requirements and emotional states. This section of the chapter may dig into self-assessment methods or procedures to assist people in recognizing indicators of stress, anxiety, or emotional discomfort.

Types of Self-Care: Physical self-care (exercise, diet, sleep), emotional self-care (self-compassion, stress management), and mental self-care (mindfulness, meditation) might all be investigated.

Creating a Self-Care strategy: This section might assist readers in developing a customised self-care strategy that is suited to their own requirements and preferences. It might entail setting objectives and developing routines.

Self-Care Obstacles: Many people find difficulties in practicing self-care. These might be external impediments such as time limits or internal barriers such as remorse. The chapter might discuss solutions for overcoming these obstacles.

Emotional Well-Being: Investigating the topic of emotional well-being may entail analyzing the significance of emotional resilience, coping mechanisms, and successful emotional regulation measures.

Practical approaches: This section of the chapter might include exercises and approaches for increasing emotional well-being. Deep breathing exercises, writing, and getting professional aid when necessary are some examples.

Self-Care requirements change between Life phases: Recognizing that self-care requirements change between life phases (e.g., adolescence, maturity, and the elderly), the chapter may include advice on changing self-care techniques accordingly.

Sharing real-life examples or case studies can assist demonstrate the advantages of self-care and emotional well-being activities.

Conclusion and Future Commitment: The chapter might close by highlighting the continuing aspect of self-care and urging readers to prioritize their emotional well-being.

CHAPTER 13 ADHD AND PHYSICAL HEALTH.

However, because you haven't identified a specific book or source, I'll offer a basic summary of the issue as it relates to ADHD and physical health.

ADHD and Physical Health is the title of this article.

Introduction: The chapter "ADHD and Physical Health" delves into the complex link that exists between Attention Deficit Hyperactivity Disorder (ADHD) and several areas of physical health. ADHD is a neurodevelopmental condition that has a significant impact on cognitive and behavioral performance. While ADHD is well-known for its effects on attention, impulsivity, and hyperactivity, this chapter digs at how ADHD may also have an affect on a person's physical well-being.

The ADHD-Physical Health Connection:

Nutrition and Diet: Diet is a crucial link between ADHD and physical health. Individuals with ADHD sometimes struggle to maintain a healthy diet. This can result in dietary deficits, especially in vital vitamins and minerals. Poor diet can aggravate ADHD symptoms and have long-term health implications.

ADHD can impair an individual's ability to engage in regular physical activity. While hyperactivity may appear to be beneficial in this sense, it can also lead to impulsive and occasionally unsafe actions during physical play. On the other side, some people with ADHD may battle with low energy and inactivity, which can lead to physical health problems including obesity.

Sleep Disorders: Many people with ADHD have trouble sleeping. These changes in sleep patterns can lead to chronic sleep deprivation, which can have a negative impact on physical health. Sleep is essential for general health, and lack of it can result in difficulties such as reduced immune function, psychological disorders, and cardiovascular problems.

ADHD frequently coexists with other mental health and physical health issues. Individuals with ADHD, for example, may be more prone to anxiety and sadness, which can have a negative influence on their overall health. Furthermore, ADHD has been linked to illnesses such as obesity, cardiovascular disease, and substance misuse.

Treatment and Management: Strategies for controlling ADHD in the context of physical health may be discussed in this chapter. These are some examples:

Medication: Stimulants and non-stimulants are routinely used to treat ADHD symptoms, which can enhance physical health indirectly by addressing behavioral and cognitive problems.

Behavioral Interventions: Behavioral treatment strategies can assist people with ADHD in developing healthier behaviors such as increased eating, frequent exercise, and better sleep hygiene.

Education and Support: Educating and supporting persons with ADHD and their families is critical for managing both the cognitive and physical elements of the illness.

Finally, the chapter "ADHD and Physical Health" investigates the multidimensional link between ADHD and physical well-being. It emphasizes the significance of comprehensive management options that address both cognitive and physical health in order to improve the overall quality of life for people with ADHD. This chapter is a helpful resource for healthcare providers, educators, and ADHD persons and families.

CHAPTER 14
PARENTING WITH ADHD:

A Balancing Act" from any source up to my most recent training data

However, based on typical subjects connected to parenting and ADHD, I can offer a basic idea of what a chapter with that title may cover:

"Parenting with ADHD: A Balancing Act" is most likely a chapter that discusses the difficulties and techniques involved in raising children when one or both parents suffer from Attention Deficit Hyperactivity Disorder (ADHD). Here's a more in-depth explanation of what such a chapter may contain:

Introduction to ADHD: The chapter would begin by defining ADHD, its many kinds (inattentive, hyperactive-impulsive, and combined), and how it manifests in adulthood.

Prevalence and Diagnosis: It may describe the prevalence of ADHD in adults as well as the diagnostic procedure, emphasizing the significance of detecting ADHD in parents.

The Effects of ADHD on Parenting: In this part, we will look at how ADHD can influence a parent's ability to handle everyday activities, routines, and obligations. It would go into the emotional and practical issues that arise.

Balancing duties: This chapter would teach parents with ADHD how to balance their own demands and duties with those of their children. This might involve time management and organizing abilities.

Communication and Relationships: It might discuss how ADHD affects family communication and offer advice on effective communication skills. It might also go over how ADHD impacts parent-child interactions.

controlling Symptoms: Strategies for controlling ADHD symptoms in the context of parenting would be critical. This might include medication, counselling, or lifestyle modifications to assist parents in better managing their illness.

Support Systems: The chapter may stress the significance of obtaining help from healthcare experts, support groups, and loved ones. It might also address the role of a spouse in good co-parenting.

Positive Parenting: It is critical to encourage positive parenting strategies such as setting clear expectations, creating structure, and delivering praise and incentives.

Self-Care: The chapter would emphasize the need of self-care for ADHD parents. It may offer suggestions on how to prioritize self-care and lessen stress.

Children's Perspective: An empathy part may investigate how children see and react to their parents' ADHD. It would go over strategies for helping youngsters comprehend and cope with the issue.

Success examples and Testimonials: Including real-life examples of ADHD parents who have successfully handled parenting problems might give motivation and relatability.

Resources: The chapter would close with a list of resources for parents to obtain further knowledge

and assistance, such as books, websites, and
organizations.

CHAPTER 15 FUTURE OUTLOOK AND LIFELONG STRATEGIES FOR ADHD PATIENTS.

However, because I lack access to specific chapters or volumes, I'll offer a general outline of what such a chapter would contain based on common knowledge up to my most recent training data. ADHD Patients' Long-Term Prospects and Strategies

This chapter dives into the long-term implications and methods for those who have Attention Deficit Hyperactivity Disorder (ADHD). It acknowledges that ADHD is a neurodevelopmental disorder that frequently continues throughout a person's life, and that it is critical to prepare for the future and apply techniques that improve general well-being and productivity.

Understanding Adhd Throughout Life:

Discussing how ADHD symptoms may progress from infancy through adolescent and maturity. Challenges at various periods of life: Identifying the special obstacles that people with ADHD may have at school, employment, and in their personal relationships.

Adolescence to Adulthood Transition:

Education and career planning: ADHD management strategies for the transition from high school to college or the workforce.

Tips for building skills in time management, organization, and self-care for independent living.

Workplace and Career Strategies:

Accommodation and disclosure: Discussing the advantages and disadvantages of reporting an

ADHD diagnosis to employers and investigating possible employment adjustments.

Time management and organization: Techniques to assist those with ADHD in excelling in their employment.

Family Life and Relationships:

Communication: Techniques for increasing communication with loved ones, such as couples and children.

The significance of developing and maintaining a solid support network.

Medication and Therapy Management:

Medication considerations: Examining the function of medication management in the treatment of ADHD across the lifetime.

Methods of treatment: Investigating the long-term advantages of different therapeutic methods, such as cognitive-behavioral therapy (CBT).

Self-Care and Well-Being Promotion:

Techniques for controlling stress and anxiety, which are frequently co-occurring with ADHD.

Exercise, diet, and sleep all have a part in treating ADHD symptoms.

Self-Advocacy and Advocacy:

Individual empowerment includes encouraging self-advocacy and spreading knowledge about ADHD in order to minimize stigma.

Community resources: Find out about support groups, advocacy organizations, and other resources in your community.

Conclusion: This chapter emphasizes the significance of treating ADHD holistically throughout the lifespan. It highlights that persons with ADHD may live full and successful lives with the right methods, support, and self-awareness. Furthermore, it emphasizes that continuous research and breakthroughs in ADHD therapy are constantly improving the prognosis for people suffering from the disorder.